Contents

Palm Tree

Size: 10¼ inches W x 24¼ inches L
(26cm x 61.6cm), including hanger
Skill Level: Intermediate

Materials

❑ 1 sheet 7-count plastic canvas
❑ Uniek Needloft plastic canvas yarn as listed
   in color key
❑ #16 tapestry needle
❑ 9 x 6mm pony beads: 38 bright pink, 6 green
❑ 19¼-inch (48.9cm) light orange acrylic
   wind twister
❑ Monofilament
❑ 1½-inch (3.8cm) white plastic ring

Stitching Step by Step

1 Cut plastic canvas according to graphs.

2 Following graphs throughout, stitch and Overcast flip-flops. Stitch leaf centers and tips following graphs. Whipstitch leaf tips to leaf centers from red dot to red dot; Overcast remaining edges.

Assembly

1 Cut a 12-inch (30.5cm) length of holly yarn. Thread length up through center of all three assembled leaves where indicated with green dot. Thread on all six green beads, wrap two times around plastic ring; go back down through beads and leaves. Thread length through hole on narrow end of wind twister and secure under leaves. Evenly space leaves apart.

2 Using orange yarn, make a small loop where indicated on each flip-flop just large enough to thread through a length of yarn.

3 Cut a 12-inch (30.5cm) length of orange yarn for each flip-flop strap. For each flip-flop, bring yarn up in hole indicated on outer side of flip-flop. Thread on 10 bright pink beads, thread through orange loop and add nine more beads, going down where indicated on inner side of flip-flop. Secure yarn on backside; trim.

4 Using monofilament throughout, tack flip-flops together as in photo. Attach flip-flops to wide end of wind twister.

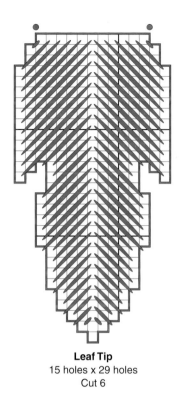

Leaf Tip
15 holes x 29 holes
Cut 6

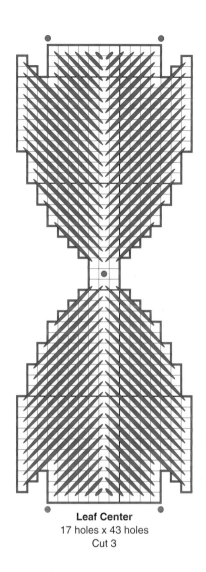

Leaf Center
17 holes x 43 holes
Cut 3

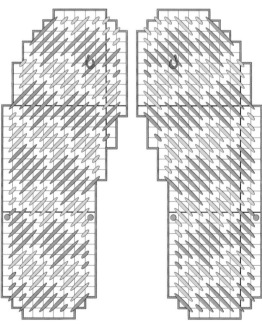

Flip-Flops
12 holes x 29 holes
Cut 1 each

COLOR KEY	
Yards	**Plastic Canvas Yarn**
75 (68.6m)	■ Holly #27
10 (9.2m)	☐ Yellow #57
20 (18.3m)	■ Bright orange #58
	◊ Attach bright orange #58 loop
	● Attach bright orange #58 strap
Color numbers given are for Uniek Needloft plastic canvas yarn.	

Hummingbird

Size: 5¼ inches W x 17 inches L
(13.3cm x 43.2cm), including hanger
Skill Level: Intermediate

Materials

❑ ½ sheet 7-count plastic canvas
❑ 5-inch Uniek QuickShape plastic canvas star
❑ 3 (6-inch/15cm) Uniek QuickShape plastic canvas radial circles
❑ Uniek Needloft plastic canvas yarn as listed in color key
❑ 6-strand embroidery floss as listed in color key
❑ #16 tapestry needle
❑ 39 (9 x 6mm) translucent pink pony beads
❑ 1½-inch (3.8cm) white plastic ring

Stitching Step by Step

1 Cut plastic canvas according to graphs (pages 5–7), cutting away gray areas on flower (star) and swirls (6-inch circles).

2 Following graphs through step 4, Overcast long curved edges of swirls over two bars as shown on graph. Stitch and Overcast flower, working yellow French Knots in center.

3 Stitch hummingbird front and back, working uncoded areas on front with mermaid Continental Stitches and uncoded areas on back with mermaid Reverse Continental Stitches.

4 When background stitching is completed, work embroidery with brown yarn and green floss. Do not Whipstitch hummingbird pieces together at this time.

Assembly

1 Following Fig. 1, with swirls going in the same direction, Whipstitch A to B, B to C; then Whipstitch C to A (along red lines), forming a point. Repeat on other end of swirls.

2 Use watermelon yarn throughout assembly. Cut an 8-inch (20.3cm) length of yarn and thread through needle. Bring needle up through stitching on back side of flower, coming out at black arrow. Thread on 8 beads, wrap yarn two times around plastic ring and bring yarn back down through beads, securing again under stitching on back side of flower; trim yarn.

3 Cut a 14-inch (35.6cm) length of yarn and bring needle down through stitching at center bottom of flower, following blue arrow. Thread on 8 beads, go down through point on one end of swirls, thread on 15 beads, bring yarn down through bottom point of swirls, thread on 8 beads, and bring yarn down through stitching on humming bird back at black arrow; trim yarn.

4 Whipstitch hummingbird front and back together following graphs, working around beading yarn at top of hummingbird wing.

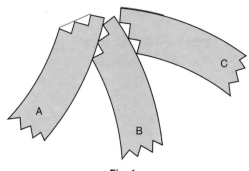

Fig. 1
Swirl Assembly

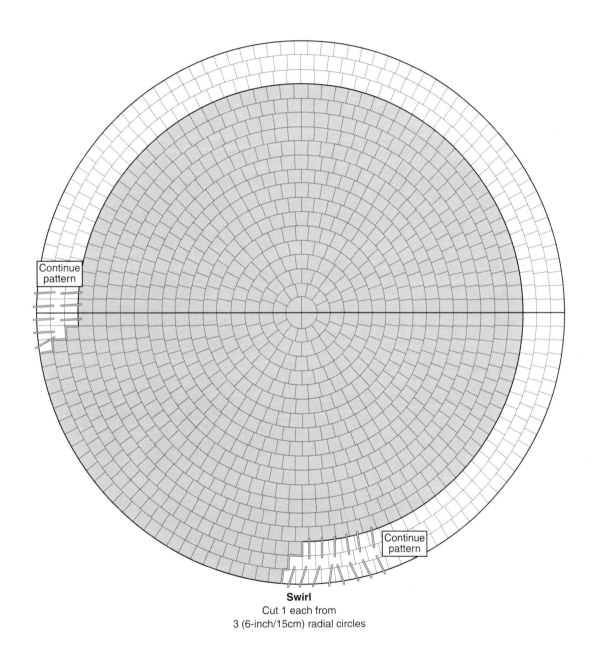

Swirl
Cut 1 each from
3 (6-inch/15cm) radial circles

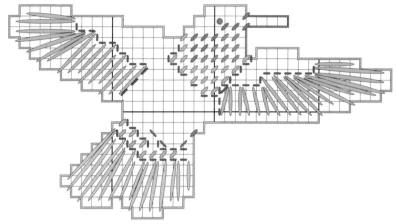

Hummingbird Front
37 holes x 20 holes
Cut 1

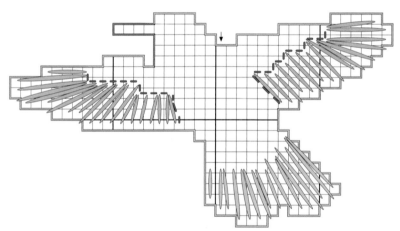

Hummingbird Back
37 holes x 20 holes
Cut 1

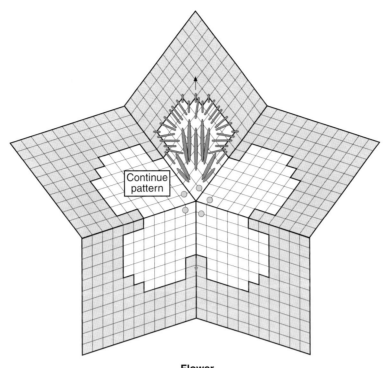

Flower
Cut 1 from 5-inch star,
cutting away gray areas

COLOR KEY	
Yards	**Plastic Canvas Yarn**
1 (1m)	■ Brown #15
25 (22.9m)	▫ Mermaid #53
10 (9.2m)	▫ Turquoise #54
10 (9.2m)	■ Watermelon #55
	Uncoded areas on humming-bird front are mermaid #53 Continental Stitches
	Uncoded areas on humming-bird back are mermaid #53 Reverse Continental Stitches
	╱ Mermaid #53 Overcast and Whipstitch
	╱ Watermelon #55 Overcast
	╱ Brown #15 Backstitch and Straight Stitch
	● Brown #15 French Knot
1 (1m)	○ Yellow #57 French Knot
	6-Strand Embroidery Floss
3 (2.8m)	╱ Green Backstitch
Color numbers given are for Uniek Needloft plastic canvas yarn.	

Heart Trio

Size: 6¾ inches W x 15¼ inches L
(17.1cm x 38.7cm), including hanger

Skill Level: Beginner

Materials

❑ 6-inch Uniek QuickShape plastic canvas heart
❑ 2 Darice 3-inch plastic canvas heart shapes #33147
❑ Plastic canvas yarn as listed in color key
❑ Iridescent craft cord as listed in color key
❑ #16 tapestry needle
❑ Beading needle
❑ Beads from Sulyn Industries Flower Garden
#88091-54 Beading Fun Pack:
  45 clear and iridescent round beads
  6 crystal bicones
  3 violet flowers
  3 violet metallic roundelles
❑ 1½-inch (3.8cm) white plastic ring

Stitching Step by Step

1 Cut plastic canvas according to graphs, cutting away gray areas.

2 Using #16 tapestry needle, Overcast hearts following graphs.

3 Use string from beading pack and a beading needle throughout assembly. Cut two 8-inch (20.3cm) lengths of string and thread through needle. Bring needle up through stitching on back side of large heart, coming out at center top at arrow. Thread on 13 round beads, wrap yarn two times around plastic ring and bring needle back down through beads, securing thread again under stitching on back side of heart.

4 Thread needle with two 24-inch (61cm) lengths of string. Bring needle down through stitching at center top of large heart, following arrow. Thread on one round bead, go down through yarn at top of one small heart at arrow, add one round bead, one bicone bead, one flower bead, one bicone bead and two round beads; go down through yarn at bottom of small heart, bringing yarn out at arrow. Add on four round beads.

5 Following arrows, bring needle down through stitching at back of large heart, coming down at bottom point and add four round beads.

6 Continue by running thread down through second small heart; adding beads to center of heart as for first small heart and bringing yarn out at bottom of heart. Add three round beads, one bicone bead, one flower bead and one bicone bead.

7 For dangles at bottom (Fig. 1), thread on five round beads and one metallic roundelle. Wrap thread around roundelle and go back up through five round beads. Repeat two more times for a total of three dangles. Bring needle up through all beads to bottom of small heart. Tie thread off and trim close to knot.

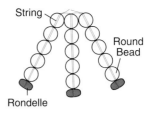

Fig. 1

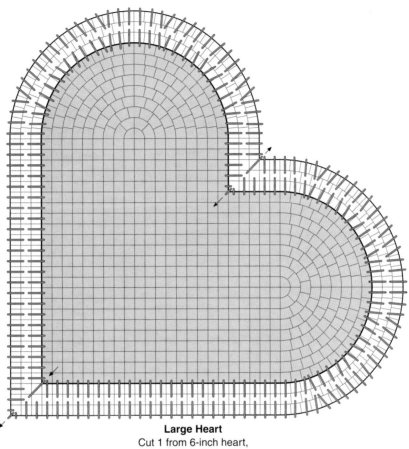

Large Heart
Cut 1 from 6-inch heart,
cutting away gray area

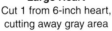

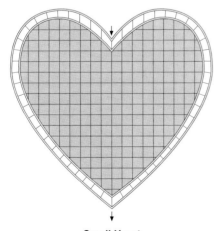

Small Heart
Cut 2 from 3-inch hearts,
cutting away gray area

COLOR KEY	
Yards	**Plastic Canvas Yarn**
9 (8.3m)	✎ Bright purple Overcast
	Iridescent Craft Cord
6 (5.5m)	✎ White Overcast

Butterfly & Dragonflies

Size: 6 inches W x 30¼ inches L
(15.2cm x 76.8cm), including hanger
Skill Level: Intermediate

Materials

❏ 1 sheet purple 7-count plastic canvas
❏ 4 (4½-inch/11.4cm) Darice plastic canvas
radial circles
❏ Uniek Needloft plastic canvas yarn as listed
in color key
❏ #16 tapestry needle
❏ Beads from Sulyn Industries Rainbow Butterflies
#88091-56 Beading Fun Pack:
  40 (5mm) round crystal faceted beads
  18 (10mm) round blue beads
  16 (10mm) round pink beads
  7 (8mm) round purple faceted beads
  6 (13 x 11mm) silver butterflies
❏ 6 (9 x 6mm) purple pony beads
❏ 7 inches (17.8cm) 22-gauge blue craft wire
❏ 1½-inch (3.8cm) white plastic ring

Stitching Step by Step

1 Cut butterfly and dragonfly pieces from purple
plastic canvas according to graphs (pages
11–13), carefully cutting out antennae and center tops
of dragonflies. One butterfly will remain unstitched for
backing.

2 Cut spiral segments from radial circles according to
graphs (pages 12 and 13), cutting away gray areas.

3 Following graphs, stitch one butterfly and four
dragonflies. To stitch center part of dragonflies,
begin at arrow and stitch up with bright purple to top.
Place one purple pony bead on post for eye and thread
yarn through bead. Place bead on remaining post and bring
yarn down through bead. Continue stitching down other
side of dragonfly center to bottom, Overcasting bottom
edge as shown to complete.

4 Beginning with first (top) spiral segment and with
royal Overcasting on the outside, Overcast curved
edges of spiral segments over two bars to middle row of
holes as shown on graphs, overlapping three holes on ends
where indicated (yellow shading) with next spiral segment.
Continue in this manner, adding on spiral segments in
numerical order, until seventh (bottom) spiral segment is
connected. Overcast ends of spiral.

Assembly

1 Use photo as a guide and string from beading pack throughout assembly. Cut two 12-inch (30.5cm) lengths of string. Bring string up through stitching on center back side of butterfly at top arrow. Thread on beads as follows: nine crystal, one blue, one pink, one blue, one crystal. Wrap yarn two times around plastic ring and bring yarn back down through beads; fasten off on back side of butterfly; trim.

2 Whipstitch unstitched backing to stitched butterfly with bright purple, working around beading at top and inserting blue craft wire under Whipstitching where indicated with arrow. Fold wire in a "U" shape and curl ends.

3 Using two 1 yard (1m) lengths of string, bring string down through stitching on center back side of butterfly at bottom arrow. Thread on beads as follows: one crystal, one blue, one pink, one blue, one crystal. Thread string down through hole indicated with green dot on top spiral.

4 Continue adding on beads and butterflies as shown in bead assembly diagram (page 13). At bottom of beads, bring thread down through one dragonfly where indicated with green dot. Fasten off and trim thread on bottom side of dragonfly.

5 Bring beads down through center of spiral.

6 Using bright purple yarn, attach remaining three dragonflies to spiral as desired.

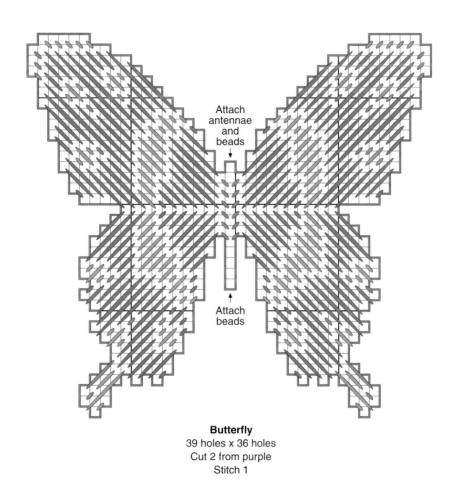

Attach antennae and beads

Attach beads

Butterfly
39 holes x 36 holes
Cut 2 from purple
Stitch 1

COLOR KEY	
Yards	**Plastic Canvas Yarn**
40 (36.6m)	■ Royal #32
30 (27.5m)	■ Bright pink #62
15 (13.8m)	■ Bright purple #64
	✏ Bright pink #62 Overcast
	✏ Bright purple #64 Overcast
5 (4.6m)	✏ White #41 Straight Stitch

Color numbers given are for Uniek Needloft plastic canvas yarn.

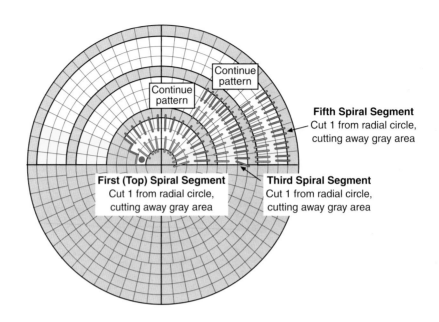

Continue pattern

Continue pattern

Fifth Spiral Segment
Cut 1 from radial circle,
cutting away gray area

First (Top) Spiral Segment
Cut 1 from radial circle,
cutting away gray area

Third Spiral Segment
Cut 1 from radial circle,
cutting away gray area

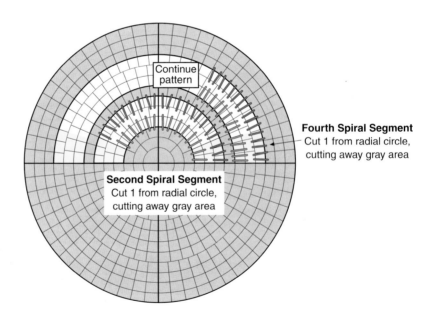

Continue pattern

Fourth Spiral Segment
Cut 1 from radial circle,
cutting away gray area

Second Spiral Segment
Cut 1 from radial circle,
cutting away gray area

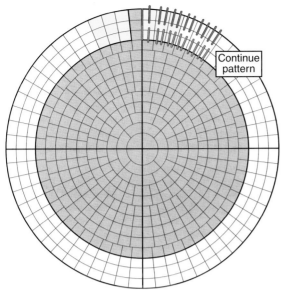

**Sixth & Seventh (Bottom)
Spiral Segments**
Cut 1 each from radial circles,
cutting away gray area

Continue
pattern

5mm round crystal faceted
10mm round blue
10mm round pink
8mm round purple faceted
13 x 11mm silver butterfly

Attach dragonfly

Bead Assembly Diagram

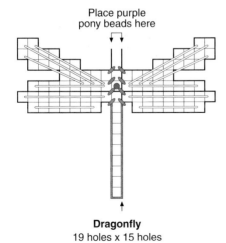

Place purple
pony beads here

Dragonfly
19 holes x 15 holes
Cut 4 from purple

COLOR KEY

Yards	Plastic Canvas Yarn
40 (36.6m)	■ Royal #32
30 (27.5m)	■ Bright pink #62
15 (13.8m)	■ Bright purple #64
	✎ Bright pink #62 Overcast
	✎ Bright purple #64 Overcast
5 (4.6m)	✎ White #41 Straight Stitch

Color numbers given are for Uniek Needloft
plastic canvas yarn.

Spiraling Hearts

Size: 8 inches W x 14 inches L
(20.3cm x 35.6cm), including hanger
Skill Level: Intermediate

Materials

- ❑ 2 (3-inch) Darice plastic canvas heart shapes #33147
- ❑ 3 (6-inch/15cm) Uniek QuickShape plastic canvas radial circles
- ❑ Plastic canvas yarn as listed in color key
- ❑ Metallic craft cord as listed in color key
- ❑ #16 tapestry needle
- ❑ 9 x 6mm pony beads: 14 white, 13 red
- ❑ 1½-inch (3.8cm) white plastic ring

Stitching Step by Step

1 Cut plastic canvas according to graphs (pages 15 and 16), cutting away gray areas on spirals (6-inch circles). Do not cut hangers from hearts.

2 Stitch and Overcast hearts following graphs. Overcast long curved edges of spirals over two bars as shown on graph.

Assembly

1 Following Fig. 1, with spirals going in the same direction and using red metallic craft cord, Whipstitch A to B, B to C; then Whipstitch C to A (along blue lines), forming a point. Repeat on other end of spirals.

2 Using a 12-inch (30.5cm) length of white yarn, bring yarn up through stitching on backside of one spiral near a point. Thread on beads as follows: white, red, white, red, white, red. Wrap yarn two times around plastic ring and bring yarn back down through beads and point of spiral.

3 Thread on a red, then white bead. Repeat beading sequence three more times. Wrap yarn around hanger on one heart and bring yarn back up through beads. Tie off under point of spiral; trim yarn close to knot.

4 Using another 12-inch (30.5cm) length of white yarn, bring yarn down through stitching on backside of one spiral near bottom point. Thread on beads as follows: white, red, white, red, white. Wrap yarn around hanger on remaining heart and bring yarn back up through beads and point of spiral.

5 Thread on a red, then white bead. Repeat beading sequence three more times. Slip yarn through Overcasting at bottom of first heart and bring yarn back down through beads. Tie off inside point at bottom of spiral; trim yarn close to knot.

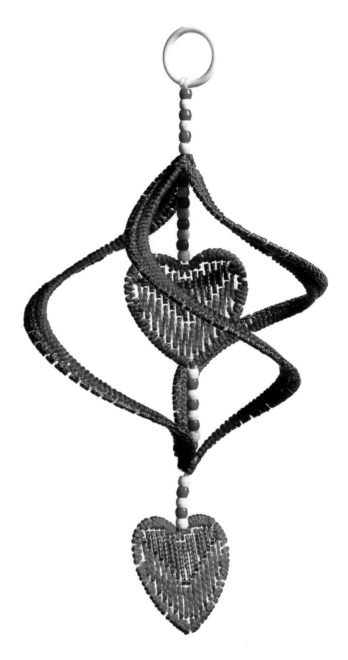

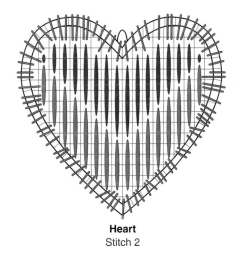

Heart
Stitch 2

COLOR KEY		
Yards	**Plastic Canvas Yarn**	
35 (32m)	▨	Red
	⁄	Red Overcast
	Metallic Craft Cord	
25 (22.9m)	▨	Red
	⁄	Red Overcast

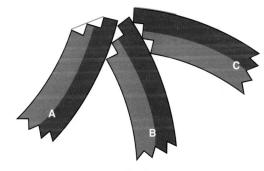

Fig. 1
Spiral Assembly

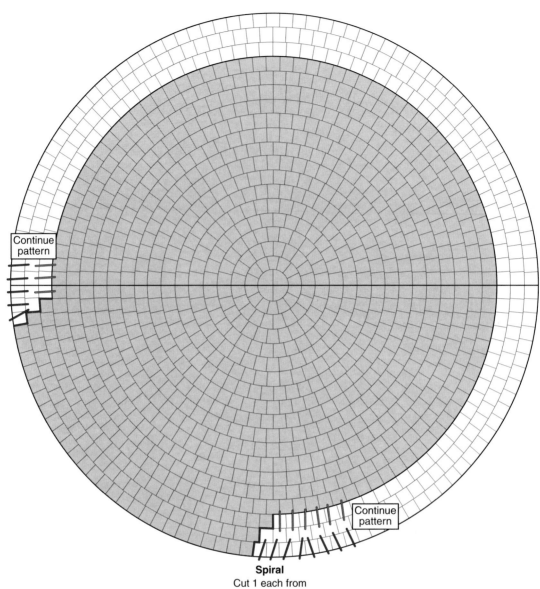

Spiral
Cut 1 each from
3 (6-inch/15cm) radial circles

COLOR KEY	
Yards	**Plastic Canvas Yarn**
35 (32m)	■ Red
	╱ Red Overcast
	Metallic Craft Cord
25 (22.9m)	■ Red
	╱ Red Overcast

Patriotic

Size: 8½ inches W x 19⅜ inches L
(21.6cm x 49.2cm), including hanger
Skill Level: Advanced

Materials

❑ 2 sheets red 7-count plastic canvas
❑ Darice 3-inch plastic canvas heart shape #33147
❑ Plastic canvas yarn as listed in color key
❑ #16 tapestry needle
❑ 9 x 6mm barrel pony beads:
    182 blue transparent
    50 red opaque
    50 white opaque

Stitching Step by Step

1 From red plastic canvas, cut the following (no graphs) for "arms" of the spinner:

2 (5-hole x 3-hole) pieces
2 (7-hole x 3-hole) pieces
6 (11-hole x 3-hole) pieces
2 (13-hole x 3-hole) pieces
2 (15-hole x 3-hole) pieces
4 (17-hole x 3-hole) pieces
4 (21-hole x 3-hole) pieces
4 (23-hole x 3-hole) pieces
2 (25-hole x 3-hole) pieces
4 (27-hole x 3-hole) pieces
6 (29-hole x 3-hole) pieces
6 (31-hole x 3-hole) pieces
2 (35-hole x 3-hole) pieces
2 (37-hole x 3-hole) pieces
2 (39-hole x 3-hole) pieces
4 (43-hole x 3-hole) pieces
4 (47-hole x 3-hole) pieces
4 (51-hole x 3-hole) pieces
4 (53-hole x 3-hole) pieces
6 (55-hole x 3-hole) pieces

2 Do not cut hanger from heart shape. Stitch and Overcast heart flag following graph (page 18).

Assembly Preparation

1 Place two of each length of spinner arms together following Fig. 1 (page 19) for placement of arm lengths, beginning with the first pair of arms (5 holes x 3 holes) and ending with the last pair of arms (7 holes x 3 holes).

2 Wrap a 2-yard (1.9m) length of red yarn around plastic ring twice, keeping tails even. Thread both tails through a red, a white, then a blue bead.

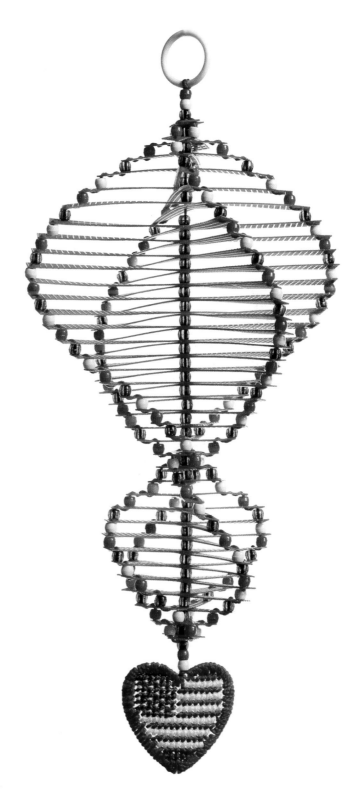

3 Following Fig. 2, thread yarn down through center hole of first pair of arms (5 holes x 3 holes). Place this pair of arms at right angles to each other. *Note: Arms are shown in different colors for clarity.*

4 Following Fig. 3, attach ends of four 2-yard (1.9m) lengths of red yarn by coming up though holes indicated with red and white dots, creating outside stringing strands. Weave yarn though holes indicated, securing ends on back side. There should now be five lengths of yarn under the assembly.

Assembly

1 Keeping both tails of center strand together throughout assembly, thread on a blue bead, the second pair (15 holes x 3 holes) of arms and another blue bead. Keep threading on pairs of arms with a blue bead between each pair, always threading yarn through center holes of arms.

2 After adding last pair of arms (7 holes x 3 holes), tighten string and temporarily tie off without cutting yarn.

3 Following Fig. 4, thread two red and two white beads on outside strands, placing same color of beads on opposite corners.

4 Following Fig. 5, place second pair of arms at right angles. Use a Running Stitch to move yarn to corners as shown. Attach two red and two white beads to corner holes under arms. *Note: Attach a red bead to yarn coming from white bead and a white bead to yarn coming from red bead.*

5 Following photo and Fig. 6 through step 6, place next pair of arms at right angles, move yarn with Running Stitches to corner holes under arms, and add blue beads.

6 Continue placing arms at right angles and adding beads, connecting to next arm with a Running Stitch and adding beads between arms, adding a blue bead every third arm until final pair of arms is reached. *Note: Beads will be placed under corner holes of smaller arms when connecting to a longer pair of arms. When connecting to a smaller pair of arms, beads will be placed above corner holes of smaller arms (see Fig. 1).*

7 Run yarn to center of arms, then thread all five lengths of yarn through a blue, red, then white bead. Wrap a couple of tails around hanger on stitched heart to connect. Secure all five lengths under yarn on back side of heart and trim.

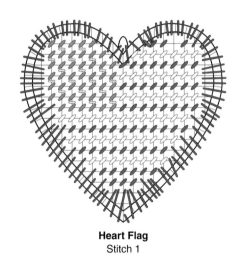

Heart Flag
Stitch 1

COLOR KEY	
Yards	**Plastic Canvas Yarn**
30 (27.5m)	■ Red
10 (9.2m)	□ White
5 (4.6m)	■ Royal blue
	✎ Red Overcast
	✎ White Running Stitch

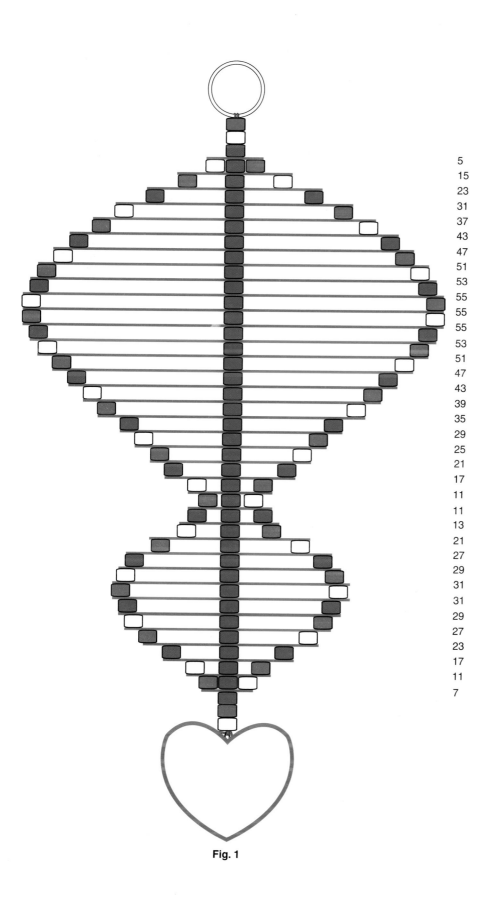

5
15
23
31
37
43
47
51
53
55
55
55
53
51
47
43
39
35
29
25
21
17
11
11
13
21
27
29
31
31
29
27
23
17
11
7

Fig. 1

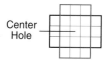

Center Hole

Fig. 2

Fig. 3

Fig. 4
View is looking
down from the top

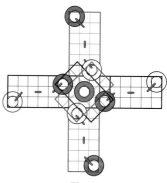

Fig. 5
View is looking
down from the top

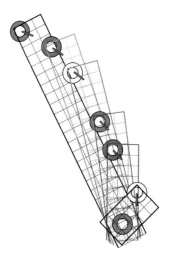

Fig. 6
Plastic canvas
shown in contrasting
colors for clarity

Dolphins

Size: 10¼ inches W x 24¼ inches L
(26cm x 61.6cm), including hanger

Skill Level: Advanced

Materials

❏ ½ sheet 7-count plastic canvas
❏ 3 (9-inch/23cm) plastic canvas radial circles
❏ Uniek Needloft plastic canvas yarn as listed
   in color key
❏ #16 tapestry needle
❏ Beads from Sulyn Industries Sparkle Dolphins
   #88091-54 Beading Fun Pack:
      101 (7mm) blue pony beads
      3 blue dolphins
      2 gray dolphins
❏ 1½-inch (3.8cm) white plastic ring

Stitching Step by Step

1 Cut plastic canvas according to graphs (pages 22 and 23), cutting away gray areas on swirls (9-inch circles).

2 Stitch two dolphins as graphed, working uncoded areas with gray Continental Stitches. Reverse remaining two dolphins before stitching, working all stitches in reverse and working uncoded areas with gray Reverse Continental Stitches.

3 When background stitching is completed, work gray Straight Stitches and French Knots.

4 Overcast curved edges of swirls over two bars with royal as shown on graphs.

Swirl Assembly

1 Use royal yarn throughout assembly. Following Fig. 1, with outer swirls going in same direction and using royal yarn, Whipstitch A to B, B to C, and C to A (along red lines), forming a point. Repeat on other end of swirls.

2 Repeat step 1 with inner swirls.

Spinner Assembly

1 Use royal yarn throughout assembly. Using a 26-inch (66cm) length of yarn, bring yarn up through stitching on backside of one swirl on outer swirls and up through top point. Thread on six blue pony beads, wrap yarn two times around plastic ring and bring yarn back down through beads and point of swirl.

2 Thread on six more blue pony beads; bring needle down through top point on inner swirls. Add six blue pony beads, one gray dolphin and three blue pony beads. Following blue arrows, bring needle down through stitching on back side of one dolphin and out at bottom edge where indicated. Whipstitch to second dolphin, working around bead at top and yarn at bottom.

3 Thread on five blue pony beads, last gray dolphin and six blue pony beads. Bring needle down through bottom point of inner swirl.

4 Following Fig. 2 through step 9, thread on nine blue pony beads, then bring needle down through bottom point of outer swirl.

5 Add six blue pony beads and bring yarn down through one hole indicated with blue dot on bottom ring; wrap yarn around edge indicated with closest red dot. Thread on 16 blue pony beads; temporarily tie off.

6 Fasten a 20-inch (50.8cm) length of yarn on bottom of ring. Bring needle up through hole indicated with second blue dot, add six beads, go up and out through bottom point of outer swirls, add on six more beads and down through last hole indicated with blue dot. Wrap around edge indicated with closest red dot.

7 Add four blue pony beads, wrap around yarn with 16 beads after fourth bead, add four blue pony beads and wrap around edge indicated with last red dot; secure yarn on bottom of ring; trim.

8 Untie yarn, thread through stitching on back of one dolphin and trim yarn; Whipstitch last two dolphins together.

9 Cut three 12-inch (30.5cm) lengths of yarn. Secure one length each around bars at green dots; going down through adjacent hole, thread on beads (eight on one length, six on second length and four on third length) and one blue dolphin; bring yarn back up through beads, securing lengths on bottom side of ring; trim.

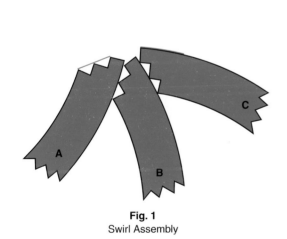

Fig. 1
Swirl Assembly

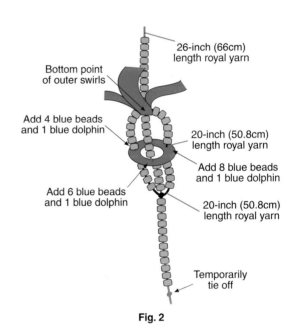

26-inch (66cm) length royal yarn

Bottom point of outer swirls

Add 4 blue beads and 1 blue dolphin

20-inch (50.8cm) length royal yarn

Add 8 blue beads and 1 blue dolphin

Add 6 blue beads and 1 blue dolphin

20-inch (50.8cm) length royal yarn

Temporarily tie off

Fig. 2

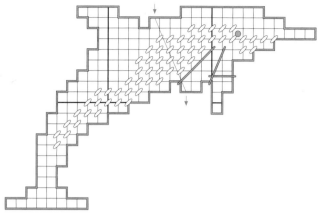

Dolphin
30 holes x 19 holes
Cut 4
Stitch 2 as graphed
Reverse 2 and work
stitches in reverse

COLOR KEY	
Yards	**Plastic Canvas Yarn**
120 (110m)	■ Royal #32
10 (9.2m)	☐ White #41
15 (13.8m)	Uncoded areas on right-facing dolphins are gray #38 Continental Stitches
	Uncoded areas on reversed (left-facing) dolphins are gray #38 Reverse Continental Stitches
╱	Gray #38 Straight Stitch and Whipstitch
●	Gray #38 French Knot
Color numbers given are for Uniek Needloft plastic canvas yarn.	

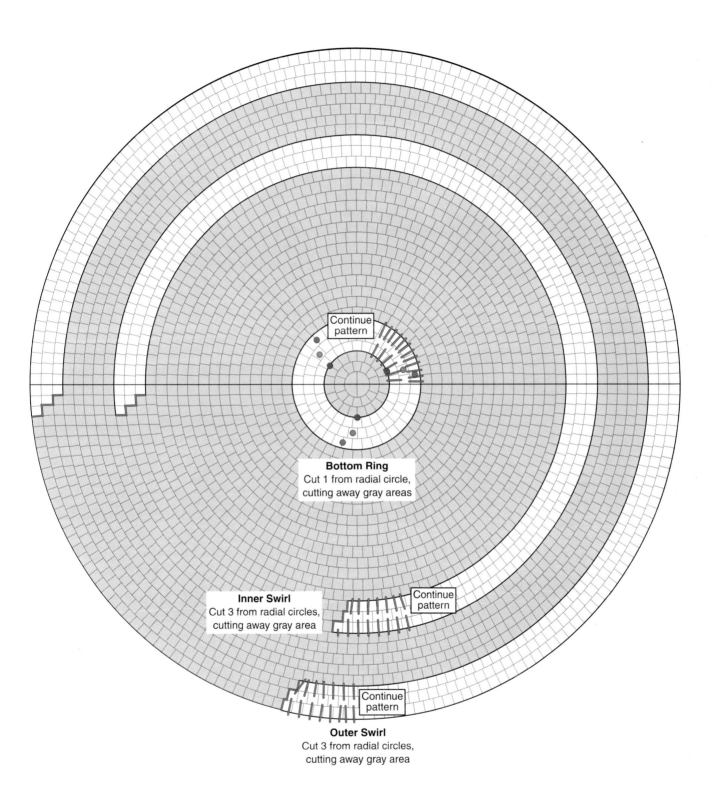

Continue pattern

Bottom Ring
Cut 1 from radial circle,
cutting away gray areas

Inner Swirl
Cut 3 from radial circles,
cutting away gray area

Continue pattern

Continue pattern

Outer Swirl
Cut 3 from radial circles,
cutting away gray area

Annie's Attic®

Wind Spinners is published by DRG, 306 East Parr Road, Berne, IN 46711. Printed in USA. Copyright © 2010 DRG. All rights reserved. This publication may not be reproduced in part or in whole without written permission from the publisher.

RETAIL STORES: If you would like to carry this pattern book or any other DRG publications, visit DRGwholesale.com

Every effort has been made to ensure that the instructions in this publication are complete and accurate. We cannot, however, take responsibility for human error, typographical mistakes or variations in individual work.

Please visit AnniesCustomerCare.com to check for pattern updates.

ISBN: 978-1-57367-349-5
Printed in USA
4 5 6 7 8 9

Shopping for Supplies

For supplies, first shop your local craft and needlework stores. Some supplies may be found in fabric, hardware and discount stores. If you are unable to find the supplies you need, please call Annie's Attic at (800) 582-6643 to request a free catalog that sells plastic canvas supplies.

Getting Started

Before You Cut

Buy one brand of canvas for each entire project as brands can differ slightly in the distance between bars. Count holes carefully from the graph before you cut, using the bolder lines that show each 10 holes. These 10-count lines begin from the left side for vertical lines and from the bottom for horizontal lines. Mark canvas before cutting; then remove all marks completely before stitching. If the piece is cut in a rectangular or square shape and is either not worked, or worked with only one color and one type of stitch, the graph is not included in the pattern. Instead, the cutting and stitching instructions are given in the general instructions or with the individual project instructions.

Covering the Canvas

Bring needle up from back of work, leaving a short length of yarn on back of canvas; work over short length to secure. To end a thread, weave needle and thread through the wrong side of your last few stitches; clip. Follow the numbers on the small graphs beside each stitch illustration; bring your needle up from the back of the work on odd numbers and down through the front of the work on even numbers. Work embroidery stitches last, after the canvas has been completely covered by the needlepoint stitches.

Basic Stitches

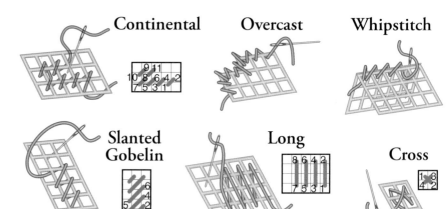

Continental Overcast Whipstitch

Slanted Gobelin Long Cross

Embroidery Stitches

French Knot

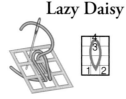
Lazy Daisy

Backstitch

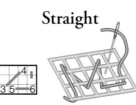
Straight

METRIC KEY:
millimeters = (mm)
centimeters = (cm)
meters = (m)
grams = (g)